Advance

Emerging Apostles & Apostolic Centers

Jonathan Ferguson

Copyright © 2014 Jonathan Ferguson

All rights reserved.

ISBN-10: 1505350700

ISBN-13: 978-1505350708

Contents

Paradigms for New Patterns 4

Apostles & Their Historical Emergence 17

The Prophetic Significance of Apostolic Emergence 27

The Administrations of Apostleship 39

The Seal, The Signs, & The Mysteries of Apostles 51

Apostolic Measures & Maturity 69

The Antioch Pattern for Apostolic Centers 80

Emerging Apostolic Centers 90

Paradigms for New Patterns

Acts 1:8
But ye shall receive power, after that the Holy Ghost is come upon you: and ye shall be witnesses unto me both in Jerusalem, and in all Judaea, and in Samaria, and unto the uttermost part of the earth.

One day, while reading the previous verse, I realized that Jesus did a lot more than promise that the believer would receive power therein. I noticed that He also gave the early Church a prophetic blueprint concerning how they would advance the Kingdom of God.

This strategy, once implemented, would cause massive growth and expansion to come to the Church. The results would in fact be that the entire planet would be touched by His presence and power by way of His Church.

It is in the light of such that I believe the anointing to revive and reclaim whole cities and nations is coming back to our generation. However, this type of anointing will require the administration of apostles and apostolic centers, which leads to my next point.

It is easy to look at Acts 1:8 and realize how the Church would touch the world, but we often overlook the changes that came about in the Church

current apostolic and prophetic community it disturbs me. It bothers me because when I read the book of Acts, I see the authentic apostolic being as "mega" as "mega" could ever be.

I think our pride keeps us from realizing that the ministries we often consider as shallow, carnal, backslidden, worldly, and the like should not be advancing more than we are if we say we have something more to offer to the world. I also think that we'd rather criticize the fruit of others instead of doing introspection and figuring out why we are not progressing in the way that we should.

Although I began this chapter bringing to light things that I believe we over look in Acts 1:8, the one thing I believe that anyone can spot out in the text is that we will have power and that we will touch the world with that power. Think about it. I will be expounding upon the apostolic and unveiling a leadership strategy that many around the world are beginning to implement and see advancement in their ministries, **BUT** if all of our apostolic revelations and strategies do not include worldwide impact and transformation what is the point?

I believe with all of my heart that the revelations God has given me to share exist as a pattern that we can utilize to once again see our world turned upside down (Acts 17:6). And although I know the apostolic represents a lot more than this, and although this book covers many more concepts than worldwide impact, the apostolic definitely does not exist without or apart from it.

However, it becomes very difficult for people to believe that God is able to save whole cities and nations in our day in time because there are not many, if any, models that point to such success. Therefore, I believe God is dealing with the Church in the same manner that He dealt with Abraham when he spoke to him concerning his seed and his mandate to father nations.

I believe God instructed Abraham to observe and count the stars and sand because as Abraham attempted at something that was virtually impossible it would challenge his perception and perspective (Genesis 15:5). Ultimately, Abraham had to be able to perceive his promise before he could conceive it. God was telling Abraham, "I'm bigger than your paradigm."

Likewise, with all of our concepts and theories concerning the apostolic, God is still saying, "I'm bigger than your paradigm." Again, one reason I believe this with all of my heart is because when the apostles were in operation in the scripture they shook whole cities and nations. I reiterate, the scripture says of them that they turned the world upside down (Acts 17:6). Notice, it didn't say they merely built successful networks and hosted annual conferences.

The Vision

I remember, in a vision once, the Lord showed me the map of America. He then asked, "How many cities do you think are represented in just one state"?

I immediately knew that there could be, at minimum, hundreds of cities represented in even the smaller states. He then said, "So you really think it's hard for me to save at least one whole major city in each state". And then He said, "And that's at minimal..."

This experience changed the way I thought about whether cities and nations could be born into the Kingdom of God in mass. It was a Genesis 15:5 moment for me in which God was stretching my faith and telling me, "I'm bigger than your paradigm."

Pressing Into More

The reality is that the apostolic mantle can labor in the Spirit for mass harvesting of souls, cities, and nations (Matthew 9:37-38). And although it seems that we have lost this element in our current apostolic movements we can apprehend this reality once again if we become the people that Psalms 24:6 speak of who seek the Lord.

In fact, Psalms 24:6 speaks more specifically of a generation that will seek the Lord—not merely a people, but a generation. It literally means, in part, that it is possible for one generation to know and seek God and the next generation to not know or seek Him necessarily.

Just think about it. In just the past 150 years we have had a Smith Wigglesworth, a Lester Sumrall, a Kenneth Hagin, a Kathryn Kuhlman and many others who were generals in God's Kingdom. They were those who changed nations as they preached the gospel, raised the dead, healed the sick, casted out devils, and etc. But now it seems that the goal of most preachers is just to have a successful ministry in the eyes of the people.

Many feel that as long as their itineraries are full, they are on Christian TV, or if they have a large following that they have arrived. And don't get me wrong, I travel extensively in ministry, I have been interviewed on the Word Network reaching over 90 million viewer and the Impact Network reaching almost 50 million.

I have best selling books, and I know there is more to come. However, if we allow these things alone to define success in God it can deceive us and cause us to lose our hunger to go after God for something more substantial in the Spirit.

Not me. I refuse. And I prophesy that if we seek the Lord there is an ancient oil of the apostolic that will return to the church. In fact, the Lord spoke to me and said, "If the current apostolic and prophetic movement does not shift into my current agenda, it will become the next pharisaical order".

That means that the very ones that fought for reformation and change on the previous front, may be the very ones to resist the reformations that are on the horizon. Therefore, I must warn you that this book may challenge your theology. But if you are up for the challenge, God is calling us to "Advance".

On What Authority am I Writing This?

Some may be reading this book and the thought is occurring, who is he to write on this subject? Well, I can validate that but I don't want to waste too much time doing so. The impartation will speak for itself. Also, I can assure you that I'm not writing something that I have heard from someone else (Galatians 1:11-12).

I have been a part of extended revivals that were in book of Acts proportion—movements that have touched thousands and attracted individuals from multiple states to gather in the location where God's Spirit was being poured out. They have shifted economies, changed government, and added hundreds to various churches. You can read testimonies of such in my book *Jesus in HD (High Demand)*.

Advance

However, the more experience in revival outbreaks you have, the more you begin to understand that they require leadership models and governing systems in order to sustain them. And if those who carry the spirit of revival are not adequately prepared for what comes "after revival" they will experience a "big splash" of God, but sadly have no remaining fruit to show for it.

The Spirit of God led me to write this book as a balancer and a propeller. He showed me that the power dimension must break into the current apostolic movement to balance its revelation with more demonstration.

Likewise, a grace for building and administration must intertwine with the current revival outbreaks of our time in order to propel what God pours out of heaven beyond the place of their current retention rates. Only then can the apostolic begin to establish lasting Kingdom cultures and create avenues from which heaven's government can be legislated in the earth.

I will touch more on these concepts later, but for now I want you to know that writing this book is not "practice" for me. I've actually seen results and have fruit in the areas that I'm writing about. Moreover, I believe that God has shown me a governing administration in the book of Acts that will be necessary in facilitating a kingdom momentum of "book of Acts" proportion.

Now that we have that out of the way, I want to get straight to the point. My goal is to lay a strong foundation of truth concerning the basics of apostleship over the next couple of chapters.

Afterwards, I want to get right into the meat of the teaching concerning apostolic centers in a "cliff notes" type of way. I don't want you to filter through a lot of fluff as you read.

Moving Forward

As we proceed in dealing with apostleship I think it is important we understand the nature of God's calling on our lives. We often miss the point when it comes to our placements and purposes among the five fold offices.

Furthermore, I believe the reason for our error is often rooted in a misconception concerning which office is the highest ranking. Because of this, we often "call" ourselves into the office that we esteem above the others, as opposed to having an authentic calling from God on our lives into a specific office of heaven's choosing.

Therefore, in conclusion of this chapter, I thought it befitting to deal with the nature of God's callings as a springboard so that as we deal with apostleship we would have prayerfully weeded out some of the craziness that attempts to attach itself to the apostolic. In doing so, I want us to simply look at

Philippians 3:14 in reference to its mentioning of the high calling of God.

I have found that if an individual has not first tamed their ambitions before reading such a verse they could easily fall prey to the immaturity of what I call "office jockeying". When individuals yield to this type of deception they treat the ministry no different than a competitive sport. Therefore, I want to look at this particular text not to dissect it theologically, but to rather inspire a way of thinking that could provide a solution to end the previously mentioned madness.

The High Callings of God

Philippians 3:14
I press toward the mark for the prize of the high calling of God in Christ Jesus.

Before I begin defining what an apostle is, I want to emphasize that the highest call is not the call to be an apostle, a prophet, a teacher, an evangelist, or a pastor. But rather that the highest calling is the call into the presence of the Lord. This is the place that the original twelve apostles were called to according to Mark 3:13-15.

I deal with this concept in my book *Prophets 101* as well. I find myself reiterating this truth a lot because I believe God wants us to understand that the world is not looking for more apostles and prophets. The earth is not waiting and travailing for the next Christian superstar, but rather for the manifestation of the sons of God according to Romans 8:19, 22.

By the way, that is the next highest calling. It is a call to be a son of God. And women, if I have to be a bride of Christ, guess what, you have to be a son of God...smile.

But on a more serious note, I think there is an urgency to understand these truths because many treat the fivefold offices as if they are some type of graduation into the Christian elite club. I don't want anyone to think that this book carries that spirit.

I want to be very clear that this book IS NOT purposed to be a confirmation to various readers of their supposed callings as an apostle. You have to understand that Jesus does not call people into this office in that manner.

Understanding, relating to, or being stirred in your spirit concerning the information you will read in this book does not give you a "green light" neither does it verify you as an apostle. You cannot use a book, a YouTube video, a personal prophecy, or any other excuse to validate you in a ministry or calling that your God assigned leadership can not verify or vouch for—but that's a side note.

I also want to be clear that those who "parade" into and around the offices are usually not those that

God has called—neither are they those who God is causing to emerge in this hour. In fact, those who will function most authentically in the apostolic office will most likely be those will not necessarily prefer the title of the apostle in front of their name.

But don't misunderstand me, the title is not always wrong and it is common for those who are beginning to awaken to the office. However, at some point we must move beyond that place.

Although there is no sin in acknowledging our offices and ranks amongst our fellow believers, we must ultimately realize that the world we are trying to reach doesn't really care. And now that we have that all cleared up I think it is safe to begin defining what the apostolic is all about without getting side tracked.

Apostles & Their Historical Emergence

What is an Apostle?

1 Corinthians 12:28
And God hath set some in the church, first apostles, secondarily prophets, thirdly teachers, after that miracles, then gifts of healings, helps, governments, diversities of tongues.

There is so much revelation concerning the apostolic that is going to emerge from this one scripture found in 1 Corinthians 12:28 that you are going to want to stay tuned in. But first let's start with the basics. What is an apostle, and where do they come from?

The History of the Apostle

In order to understand the extent of the apostolic you have to first understand where the word apostle was derived. In doing so, you will first discover that the word apostle takes on more of a significance historically than we often acknowledge in our apostolic teachings.

The truth is that the word apostle was a word used by Alexander the Great describing the individuals who were responsible for acclimating a nation to the customs and protocols of Alexander's Kingdom. Whenever Alexander had conquered territory, apostolic teams were afterward sent out to establish jurisdiction within a nation that had been conquered in war.

The sending of an apostle by a King meant that one Kingdom had been overthrown and another was now taking over. This is basically why apostles came into existence in a nutshell. You can do more study on it if you'd like.

However, in the meantime, the previous fact means that 500 years before Jesus was born, the word apostle had already gained cultural significance and relevance. Furthermore, the apostles of Jesus were introduced to the world 3 years before the church was even established.

The significance of such is that when the people heard the word apostle they did not think "clergy", but rather "diplomat". The people also knew that an apostle did not show up unless the Kingdom that they represented had already come to take over.

This is why when Jesus sent the apostles He didn't instruct them to preach that the Kingdom was coming but that the Kingdom of God was already at Hand. Let's look at a great example of this seen in Luke 10:17-19.

Luke 10:17-19

And the seventy returned again with joy, saying, Lord, even the devils are subject unto us through thy name. And he said unto them, I beheld Satan as lightning fall from heaven. Behold, I give unto you power to tread on serpents and scorpions, and over all the power of the enemy: and nothing shall by any means hurt you.

Jesus was basically informing the apostles that the reason that they had so much success in casting out devils and etc. is because He had already seen the demonic systems that were established in the regions that they were sent to preach in overthrown. Jesus only sent the apostles to announce that the Kingdom of God had come to the regions that it had in fact come into.

Therefore, the problem with our apostolic movement today is that we go into regions, establish churches, and tag the title of an apostle to our names, but it carries little weight because we have not first taken back our cities and claimed them for the Kingdom of God. The results are that there is no true apostolic foundation laid on which a strong church can be built (Matthew 16:18; Ephesians 2:20).

There are many foundational truths that I cover concerning this reality in my book *Jesus in HD (High Demand)*. For now, you get the idea that I'm trying to convey enough to move forward.

Defining an Apostle

Although I could, I'm not going to attempt to give an exhaustive definition of what an apostle is because there are many foundational books that could be studied in order to discover such. However, I will give a brief definition and revelation from scripture. Afterwards, I will go into a little more detail explaining what apostles are capable of and how it correlates with the emergence of apostolic centers.

An apostle by definition is an ambassador, a delegate, a special messenger, a sent one, or one commissioned with miraculous power. In other words, they are not only sent, but they are sent with diplomatic immunities and they are given power to validate that the special message they have been sent to deliver is indeed from the Lord.

Luke 9:52 goes into more detail to show that these sent ones are sent directly from the face of Jesus. This means that the apostolic office is not one that is self-appointed, but one in which an individual is inaugurated into the office directly by the Lord. This is why many modern apostles are often those who have testimonies of face to face encounters with Jesus similar to how the scriptures mention four specific times in which the Lord appeared to Paul validating his apostleship (Acts 26:16; Acts 18:9-10; Acts 22:17-18; Acts 23:11).

This is significant because modern day apostles not only have innumerable companies of angels that may be assisting them in ministry, but they also deal directly with the Lord Himself. Their authority is delegated directly by Jesus and then afterward endorsed by men who have credibility and examinable fruit in their offices as an apostle as well.

Jesus the Head of the Church

The apostolic verifies the reality of how closely Jesus is still interacting with the world today, through His church, even after His resurrection and ascension. He is still the head of His church and He has sent us in the same manner that the Father has sent Him. Lets look at John 20:21 and John 5:17:21 for clarity in this truth.

John 20:21
Then said Jesus to them again, Peace be unto you: as my Father hath sent me, even so send I you.

John 5:17-21
But Jesus answered them, My Father worketh hitherto, and I work. (18) Therefore the Jews sought the more to kill him, because he not only had broken the sabbath, but said also that God was his Father, making himself equal with God. (19) Then answered Jesus and said unto them, Verily, verily, I say unto you, The Son can do nothing of himself, but what he seeth the Father do:for what things soever

he doeth, these also doeth the Son likewise. (20) For the Father loveth the Son, and sheweth him all things that himself doeth:and he will shew him greater works than these, that ye may marvel. (21) For as the Father raiseth up the dead, and quickeneth them; even so the Son quickeneth whom he will.

It's one thing to know we are sent according to John 20:21 but John 5:17-19 puts the icing on the cake as to how the sending is actually played out. It is simply that apostles and apostolic people are those who simply see and hear what Jesus is doing, desires to do, or say, and afterwards are sent by Him to act out accordingly.

This is how Jesus was sent by the Father according to John 5:17-21. He was sent doing and saying everything He saw or heard the father doing or saying. He then commissions us to the same degree in John 20:21 to do and say whatever we see and hear Him doing and saying. It's really that simple. It is exactly what Mark 16:20 means concerning the apostles working with the Lord after His resurrection.

1st Apostles: Succession & Rank

1 Corinthians 12:28
And God hath set some in the church, first apostles, secondarily prophets, thirdly teachers, after that

miracles, then gifts of healings, helps, governments, diversities of tongues.

We have to understand "1st Apostles" is not merely the rank, but the order in which these offices were instituted in the church according to the historical account within the book of act. Although the office gifts were released at Jesus' ascension according to Ephesians 4:7-11, they did not emerge within the Church until the appointed time. The following list consists of the progression by which apostles, prophets, teachers, and lastly evangelist emerged successively:

Acts 1:24-26- the 12 apostles
Acts 11:27 - apostles and prophets
Acts 13:1-2 - apostles, prophets, & teachers
Acts 21:8 - evangelists

Notice that pastors were not even mentioned in the book of Acts. The reason is that it's mantle was not needed to be in play until the ground work of the church, that is featured in the book of Acts, had been laid. However, this does not diminish the importance of the pastor one bit.

I will explain this historical emergence of the fivefold gifting a little more in the following chapter. For now, I only want to refute the assumed supremacy of those who profess the apostolic office for no other reason than a desire to usurp unauthorized authority over others. This is demonic and not the spirit in which Paul writes referencing the offices as 1st, 2nd, and 3rd in the 1 Corinthians 12:28.

Therefore, although apostles are ranked first in succession, the weight of their authority is yet determined by their measure of rule within the specific sphere they are called to (2 Corinthians 10:13-16). This means that a teacher in their sphere could actually carry more weight and authority than an apostle in their particular sphere depending on how they have matured and grown into their mantle.

If apostles were indefinitely always ranked first among other fellow ministers it would leave the church to be governed by the "so called" highest ranking apostle and that would be ludicrous. That's not how the original church at Jerusalem was set up according to the book of Acts.

The founding church in fact had twelve governing apostles. And the more the leadership structure of the church evolved in the book of Acts, the more it was inclusive of additional leadership types that had governing rights outside of the apostleship.

In fact, you can always measure the maturity of an apostle who is willing to submit to the accountability of the other governing apostles and elders of the Lord's church. I reiterate that the truth is that many have tagged "apostle" to their names only in an attempt to usurp authority in the Lord's church in ways that are spiritually illegal.

Pioneers

However, in addition to the previous, "first apostles" have a lot to do with the grace on their lives to pioneer new territory and blaze new trails. Apostles don't follow trends they create culture. They are some of the most innovative and creative individuals that you will ever come across.

They are divine "solutionists" (I made up that word...pretty apostolic don't you think...smile...but back to a more serious note...). They make ways where there are no ways. Instead of seeing problems they see answers and instead of seeing chaos they see opportunity.

They are divine strategists, kingdom consultants, and spiritual advisors. They have an ability to break through spiritual resistance and plow through spiritually hard terrains.

They are able to turn a wilderness into a paradise and a desert into a garden. They can make something out of nothing. They are initiators and they are finishers. Their mantles pack everything they need in order to follow through with any given project or assignment until the desired end is completely established and adequately fortified.

I can go on and on, but at this point I believe we have enough foundation to move forward. We are going to look back at 1 Corinthians 12:28 again throughout the next chapter and dissect it more.

As we proceed, my objective is NOT to teach on the apostolic in mere theoretical or conceptual ideas derived from the definition of the word apostle. I want to rather look at and dissect what the scriptures explicitly teach concerning the apostolic mantle.

The Prophetic Significance of Apostolic Emergence

In this chapter I am going to further examine the teachings of 1 Corinthians 12:28 for two reasons. One, the historical facts surrounding the writing of the text is where I will gather the prophetic significance of apostolic emergence. Two, the details of the text examined will also lay a very strong foundation in understanding very specific administrations of the apostolic that I will cover throughout the next chapter.

I must warn you that the teaching within this chapter will be very "meaty". If you are not familiar with high levels of revelation coupled with heavy loads of facts from the scripture you may want to be sure you are reading this over and over again so that you are grasping the truths that are being presented.

However, just don't get stuck. If you find yourself consistently challenged with a particular portion as you read, don't just keep going over the same paragraph over and over, but rather keep reading while being sure you come back to revisit what needs to be revisited. Some things you'll read in the latter part of the writing may prove to be helpful in bringing understanding to some of the truths you may have stumbled over in earlier portions of this writing.

The following teachings concerning the emergence of the apostolic will give us great insights into understanding the actual administrations of the apostolic that I will cover in detail over the next chapter. So put your thinking cap on and pay close attention.

The 5-fold Ministry or the 8-fold Ministry?

1 Corinthians 12:28
And God hath set some in the church, first apostles, secondarily prophets, thirdly teachers, after that miracles, then gifts of healings, helps, governments, diversities of tongues.

Here the scripture only mentions 3 of the 5-fold offices along with 5 of the administrations that accompany those offices, which are miracles, gifts of healing, government, helps, and diversities of tongues. And I know you may be wondering where I came up with this so let me expound.

In 1 Corinthians 12:28, there is clearly a list 8 when dealing with the fivefold ministry. And in Ephesians 4:11, there is clearly a list of 5. Let's take a quick look at both.

Ephesians 4:11
And he gave some, apostles; and some, prophets; and some, evangelists; and some, pastors and

teachers;

1 Corinthians 12:28
And God hath set some in the church, first apostles, secondarily prophets, thirdly teachers, after that miracles, then gifts of healings, helps, governments, diversities of tongues.

If you compare Ephesians 4:10-11 with 1 Corinthians 12:28, you have to ask yourself is there a five-fold ministry or an eight-fold ministry. The answer is obviously that there is a fivefold ministry not an eightfold ministry.

The next question would be why would Paul expound upon some of the administrations that accompany the fivefold offices? The answer is simply this:

The context of 1 Corinthians 12:28 is 1 Corinthians 12:1. Therefore, you must understand 1 Corinthians 12:28 in light of what 1 Corinthians 12:1 is communicating. Let's take a look at the scripture and from there expound.

1 Corinthians 12:1
Now concerning spiritual (gifts), brethren, I would not have you ignorant.

Notice that the word "gifts" is italicized in the text (when reading the KJV), which means that it was not in the original text. Therefore, the text actually reads, "Now concerning the spiritual I would not have you ignorant".

Furthermore, the word spiritual is in reference to the supernatural, which means that the text is actually saying that God did not want us ignorant of the supernatural. This means that 1 Corinthians 12 is not merely a spiritual gifts teaching, but rather a teaching on the supernatural, although it does mention the spiritual gifts in context of the supernatural.

Now with that in mind we have to jump down to verse 4-6 of the text in order to understand what God did not want us ignorant of concerning the supernatural. The answer is found in three distinct dimensions of the supernatural clearly mentioned in 1 Corinthians 12:4-6 as follows: gifts, administrations, and operations. Lets look at it all together.

1 Corinthians 12:1, 4-6
(1) Now concerning spiritual (gifts), brethren, I would not have you ignorant. (4) Now there are diversities of gifts, but the same Spirit. (5) And there are differences of administrations, but the same Lord. (6) And there are diversities of operations, but it is the same God which worketh all in all.

You see, there are three dimensions of the supernatural that Paul did not want us ignorant of. Therefore, if we reduce the whole chapter of 1 Corinthians 12 to be a spiritual gifts teaching, we will end up with a little over a 30% comprehension rate of what the text is trying to convey. The chapter is actually dealing with administrations and operations of the supernatural in addition to the spiritual gifts.

In my book, *Experiencing God in the Supernatural Newly Revised*, I deal with this in more detail, and I explain the difference between the gifts, administrations, and operations. You will need to get the eBook if you want to look more into this subject.

However, what I want to bring to light here is that the five-fold ministry is where the "administrations of the Lord" come into play (1 Corinthians 12:5). It is in fact the Lord who ascended and delegated five offices according to Ephesians 4:7-11.

The gifts of the Spirit are, however, administered by the Spirit of God (1 Corinthians 12:4, 11). It is key to distinguish this because just as the Holy Ghost administers various gifts to function within the believer, the Lord Jesus also authorizes various administrations to accompany those who stand in His offices. Now, let's make more sense of this.

With the previous in mind, it is very obvious that by the time we reach vs. 28 of 1 Corinthians 12, the scripture is no longer dealing with the gifts of the spirit, but rather the administrations of the Lord. Let's look at the text again.

1 Corinthians 12:28
And God hath set some in the church, first apostles, secondarily prophets, thirdly teachers, after that miracles, then gifts of healings, helps, governments, diversities of tongues.

Now I know you are maybe thinking that the text is actually dealing with a mixture of the administrations and the gifts of the Spirit. And I do understand your logic because miracles, gifts of healing, and diversities of tongues sound like spiritual gifts to me as well.

The only problem would be where do governments and helps fit among the gifts of the Spirit if that were true? The truth is that they don't fit in at all.

Therefore, the mystery in understanding the administrations listed in 1 Corinthians 12:28, without getting them confused with the spiritual gifts, is in understanding that when an individual is operating in their office there are various administrations and clusters of gifts that accompany them in that office. Selah (Read that over again and then afterward proceed.).

For example, an individual who occupies the office of the prophet would most likely be more prone to operate in a cluster of gifts that include discerning of Spirits, word of knowledge, word of wisdom, and the gift of prophecy at bear minimal.

However, there are other administrations such as intercession and interpretation of dreams that also accompany the prophetic office that are not classified among the gifts of the Spirit. And of course there will also be administrations of governments and helps that accompany the prophetic office.

Yes, it's a mystery, but no, it's not unbiblical. The more you understand the fivefold office the more you will understand the administrations of the Lord.

The Emergence of the 5-Fold Offices

Understanding the administrations of the Lord will make more sense as you are absolutely clear on the fact that there are only 3 of the 5-fold offices mentioned in the 1 Corinthians 12:28. You would next need to likewise understand that THERE IS A REASON that only 3 of the 5-fold offices are mentioned in the 1 Corinthians 12:28. Let me explain.

Out of the fivefold offices, three of the five are primary, and 2 of the three are foundational. According to Ephesians 2:20 the two foundational offices are the offices of the apostle and prophet.

They are indeed foundational because they are responsible for securing the foundational truths upon which the church is built as mentioned in Hebrews 6:1-5.

However, the three primary of the fivefold offices are the apostle, the prophet, and the teacher. This becomes easier to embrace as you understand that although Jesus delegated these fivefold offices at His ascension, according to Ephesians 4:7-11, they actually gradually emerged on the basis of their need in the New Testament church.

I want to clarify what I mean by this by reiterating that history shows how the office of the apostle was the first to emerge in the New Testament church's leadership as we read the first couple of chapters of the book of Acts. The prophets do not join the apostles until Acts 11:27 and afterwards the teachers in Acts 13:1-2.

You have to understand that by the time Paul goes to Corinth in Acts 18:1 to establish the Corinthian church there are only 3 of the 5 offices that had emerged. The office of the evangelist does not surface until a couple of chapters, in Acts 21, and the pastor is not even listed in the book of Acts chronicles.

Prophetic Significance of the Historical Emergence

Whether you want to think of the office of the apostle, prophet, and teacher as the three primary or not really does not matter. That's just my best way of describing this truth as of now.

However, scripture does clearly show how the apostle and prophet are the foundational offices (Ephesians 2:20). And in addition to that, we cannot ignore the historical significance of the timeline in which the three offices of the apostle, prophet and teacher came into existence.

The truth is that these ministry offices did not emerge historically until the demand called for them to do so. And by the time the book of Acts lands at Antioch in Acts 13:1, the leadership structure that had begun with just apostles in Jerusalem had evolved and consisted of apostles, prophets, and teachers.

Therefore, it would make sense for Paul to elaborate on the fivefold ministry functions in using the primary three offices to illustrate the truths that he expounded on in 1 Corinthians 12:28. His very ministry had been confirmed within this Antioch structure of leadership, as seen in Acts 13:1-2, prior to him advancing to Corinth in Acts18:1.

In other words, the three offices were what the people could most relate to in explaining their administrations and doing so with a clear relevance. Paul was explaining the fivefold ministry and their administrations in 1 Corinthians 12:28 using Antioch as a model.

And the previous reveals what I believe to be a problem the church has been running into in attempting to explain the apostolic. It is that the church has been trying to explain, in theory, a dimension of the apostolic that it has not actually seen actively modeled in modern times.

The church has not seen enough of "the Bible kind of apostolic" in operation with scriptural and spiritual weight and significance. And the truth of the matter is that you don't have full revelation into something that you do not have in operation. But thanks be to God that there is greater weight of the apostolic anointing emerging.

With the previous in mind, we can now get some further clarity concerning the apostolic that is more biblically based instead of being based in mere definition derived theories. Don't get me wrong, the definitions are great, but there has to be a more solid biblical description of the apostolic. I believe this book is merely a piece of that reality.

God is giving us more insight into the apostolic because there is and there is coming a stronger weight of it in operation in the earth. It's not the apostolic in word but in deed.

It's the type of apostolic anointing that carries the results of the book of Acts. That's what's here and that's what's coming. Because, sad to say, after all of our apostolic and prophetic conferences we have yet to see such.

If we are not willing to admit that, we are only deceiving ourselves. However, I do not write this in utter disrespect of that which has gone before us and paved the way concerning the apostolic.

I believe that a great foundation has been laid and I believe that what God is raising up is because of those that have pioneered and paved the way and introduced the office of the apostle back to a world that believed that the apostolic died with the original 12.

So, before we proceed, I do want to honor those who have paved the way, while in the same breath, prophetically announce that we cannot merely camp out in the progress we have made so far. And I pray that this is provoking you.

I also pray that if you are a professing apostle and this has upset you so far that you would at least have enough courage to keep reading. I just believe that if we are going to profess apostleship we should at least want to see Bible results.

Our apostleship should look like the book of Acts and more because where the original apostles ended is where we started. We are supposed to go higher. The ceiling for the apostles in the book of Acts should be our floor, or we should have enough integrity to remove the titles from our names.

The Administrations of Apostleship

So far there is a ton of revelation that has come forth as we have examined 1 Corinthians 12:28. However, all of the previous has only served as foundational to get us where we are now. At this point, we are going to look at the scripture again and discover truths concerning the apostolic that I believe are often overlooked.

1 Corinthians 12:28
And God hath set some in the church, first apostles, secondarily prophets, thirdly teachers, after that miracles, then gifts of healings, helps, governments, diversities of tongues.

Notice that what immediately follows the office of the teacher in the text is miracles. Afterwards there are gifts of healing, helps, governments, and tongues.

More importantly, also notice that neither of the previous that follow the office of the teacher in the text are fivefold offices. And the following revelation is what you need to brace yourself for if you are one that has not read the previous chapter prior to reading this chapter.

The revelation is that everything mentioned after the office of the teacher in 1 Corinthians 12:28 are administrations that accompany the office of the apostle. They are in fact the "power packaging" by which the apostle's mantle derives its key functions.

This is not to imply that the five additional administrations mentioned in 1 Corinthians 12:28 do not accompany any other fivefold office, but rather that I want to focus solely on the apostolic office. If you are having problems accepting this truth you may want to read the previous chapter to discover where this revelation derives from. Afterwards feel free to come back to this chapter and pick up where you left off.

At this point, I want to move forward and expound upon some of the specific administrations that 1 Corinthians 12:28 mentions in reference to the apostle. In fact, I'm going to take the remainder of this chapter in order to do just that. You will find that as I expound on each of these accompanying five administrations you will better understand what an apostle is called and anointed to do.

However, I must warn you that you may notice my writing style somewhat drastically changing after this point. The reason is that, and I reiterate, I'm not interested in filling paragraphs with fluff, but rather getting straight to the point.

Power Gifts & Governments

The power gifts and governments play a major role in the administrations and functions of the apostolic mantle. Let's explore.

1 Corinthians 12:28
And God hath set some in the church, first apostles, secondarily prophets, thirdly teachers, after that miracles, then gifts of healings, helps, governments, diversities of tongues.

Miracles & Gifts of Healing

Apostles have power gifts to establish and enforce what Jesus is doing in any given area and at any given time.

They manifest and legislate the heavens in the earth by way of miracles, signs, and wonders.

Apostles demonstrate in power that the kingdom of God has come to a particular area. They do this because the Kingdom is simply when things come "in earth as they are in heaven" (Matthew 6:10).

And because there are no sicknesses, no devils, no poverty, and no sin in heaven, apostles have power to move these things out of the territories that they have been called to advance God's Kingdom in (See also Romans 15:19). Let's take a look at 2 Corinthians 12:12.

2 Corinthians 12:12
Truly the signs of an apostle were wrought among you in all patience, in signs, and wonders, and mighty deeds.

Notice, in 2 Corinthians 12:12 it didn't say that the sign or mark of the apostle is merely miracles, but rather that the signs of an apostle are wrought in miracles. This understanding is key because there are many works that are predominantly supernatural in nature that marks an individual to be an apostle and should be considered as signs of an apostle in addition to signs and wonders. We will cover many of these works in the following chapter.

In other words, all of the works that an individual does that marks them as an apostle are wrought in miracles, signs, perseverance, and mighty deeds according to 2 Corinthians 12:12. Therefore, we should understand that the apostolic is not merely in signs and demonstration, but requires the power gifts in order to break into regions and establish what needs to be established.

This is not in any way to minimize the importance of power. There is no apostolic apart from the demonstration of God's power and spirit.

However, I reiterate that there are many works that apostles accomplish in addition to miracles, signs, and wonders. And they, in fact, accomplish these works in power and in the demonstrations of God's Spirit. We will get into those works specifically as we deal with the seal of apostleship.

Other Administrations of Apostleship

1 Corinthians 12:28
And God hath set some in the church, first apostles, secondarily prophets, thirdly teachers, after that miracles, then gifts of healings, helps, governments, diversities of tongues.

Helps, Governments, & Tongues

Apostles have gifts of government, helps, and tongues in order to clearly articulate, bring structure to and adequately administrate the move of God.

The way that this works is that when there is a move of God apostles can assess it, in order to determine what systems and structures need to be set in place, in order to properly facilitate what is taking place to the end that it is completely established and not lost or forfeited.

Afterward, further assessments are made in order to implement systems that promote the continual progressions and advancement of the Kingdom through the church.

However, in order to bring government and order, apostles have to first be able to clearly articulate the move of God in which government is intending to be established. Peter preaching in the upper room on the day of Pentecost is a great example of this faculty of the apostolic.

Acts 2:14-16
But Peter, standing up with the eleven, lifted up his voice, and said unto them, Ye men of Judaea, and all ye that dwell at Jerusalem, be this known unto you, and hearken to my words: (15) For these are not drunken, as ye suppose, seeing it is but the third hour of the day. (16) But this is that which was spoken by the prophet Joel;

Notice that Peter was not preaching in attempt to initiate or incite a move of God, but rather preaching to articulate the move that had already come (Acts 2:1-4). Therefore, as similar apostles emerge, we will notice the preaching platform change in the body of Christ.

It will change because there are many great preachers who can orate a good sermon in hopes of a move of God being released in result, but there are few of those who's preaching cooperates with, compliments, and articulates the exact movements of the Spirit at hand.

Many still believe that the height and pinnacle of their preaching is some type of response from the people whether in be in their celebration or their response to an altar call. However, apostolic preaching carries more weight than that. Through it, Peter was able to clearly articulate the move of God that had hit the upper room, and in result, 3000 were added to the church.

Furthermore, Peter was only able to articulate the move of God because he actually embodied the move of God. Apostles don't preach what they don't carry. This is why when they bring a message it is not for explanation, but in demonstration and power of the Spirit (1 Corinthians 2:4).

More on Governments & Helps

Apostles' mantles are agile enough to progressively establish prophetic grids, models, and templates around the current moves of God while also fortifying kingdom strongholds to solidify the old.

Jesus taught them the importance of such in explaining the proper stewardship of both new & old wine (Luke 5:37-38). The wine represents the flow of the Spirit and the wineskin or wine bottle represents the methodologies and operations through which the Flow of the Spirit is expressed.

The problem with the teaching is that we often mention the dangers of storing new wine in old wineskins, but rarely mention the reason why Jesus taught such. Jesus clearly taught that placing old wine in old wineskins and new wine in new wineskins would preserve both the old wine and the new wine together (Luke 5:38). Jesus did not imply in any way that the new wine was maybe in some way better than old wine.

You see, apostles have to be able to construct new wineskins and models of ministry while at the same time preserving the old. This is partly what their grace for helps and governments exist to create.

Their mantles are designed to merge the power, glory, and principals of the ancient with the innovative methodologies and strategies of both the modern and the next. Their mantles are built to be "more than relevant" and they demonstrate it without the risk of compromising to the trends of the world's cultures.

This is one of the supernatural abilities that the works of an apostle are wrought in according to 2 Corinthians 12:12 in addition to mighty works, signs, and wonders. Everything they do houses the power to both author and finish a particular work.

On one spectrum they can preserve what has been and secure the foundations of old, and on the other spectrum they bring into existence things that have not been causing the church to advance beyond the times. We discover this revelation in the definition of the word patience in the text. Let's take a look at it.

2 Corinthians 12:12
Truly the signs of an apostle were wrought among you in all patience, in signs, and wonders, and mighty deeds.

Note: Patience - endurance, preservation & continuance

You see…the patience of an apostle is not just the ability to stick to something, but rather also to progress in a thing. Therefore, apostles create systems that administrate both the preservation of what is and the progression into what is to be.

Apostles understand there are many models through which the kingdom of God is expressed and that the administration and government of the church must constantly adjust to accommodate the progressive moves of the Spirit. Their mantles immediately adjust to the demands and communicates the wisdom necessary to advance.

The following consists of four examples of the leadership structure of the church evolving. You will discover that such requires an apostolic grace of helps and governments.

Study the following scriptures and I will elaborate momentarily:
1) Acts 1:24-26 & Acts 2:42
2) Acts 6:1
3) Acts 13:1 & Acts 15:22

In each previous example, the administration and government of the church shifted apostolically. The template and model of leadership changed.

What we learn from this is that every fresh wind of the Spirit requires an adequate accompanying administration in order for its progression to be preserved.

Churches die when they don't progress. And it can be very frustrating to welcome change, but not have the leadership capacity to steward it, hence one of the necessities of the apostolic.

Furthermore, the previous progression of leadership systems as shown in the book of Acts also prophetically reveals levels and tiers of apostolic leadership as follows:

Jonathan Ferguson

3 Tiers of Apostolic Leadership

1) The 1st tier is apostolic governance. (Acts 1:24-26; Acts 2:42)

2) The 2nd tier is administration and helps (Acts 6:1)

3) The 3rd and highest tier is apostolic teams, apostolic companies, and apostolic councils (Acts 13:1; Acts 15:22)

Although the concept is rather new for many, I want to emphatically inform you that the maturity of the apostle can be measured by what previous levels of government they are willing to comply with. In fact, the higher an individual ascends into apostleship the more accountability and teamwork is required, which is why the last and highest tier mentioned includes apostolic council.

Team Counsel

True apostles have a team spirit and gathers with other apostles and elders for counsel at prophetic round tables in various cities, regions, and nations. Apostles also maintain an attitude that welcomes the wisdom of other apostles from different spheres and locations (Acts 15:6; Acts 13:1). True apostles understand that they do not "have it all" and they are not striving to be the "most anointed".

Advance

In fact, the ability to form a team council is one of the key foundational patterns that must be in place when establishing what I refer to as an apostolic center. It is a place where regional spiritual authority is exercised, multitudes can gather for corporate worship and training, strategies are released to claim more territory for the Kingdom of God, and where believers can be trained to harvest their particular spheres and arenas.

I believe that "The Ramp" in Hamilton, AL, was one of the closest examples that God was constructing of such a place before it became a local church. I believe its focus towards citywide, regional, and eventually national revival was a seed of what an apostolic center represents.

And the reason I emphasize a seed is because the next step after revival is to then disciple nations. This is where and when even governments and kings begin to submit to the wisdom of God via the church, but this requires a team council in order to execute.

This is some of what these emerging apostolic centers will facilitate. With that in mind, we are almost at the place where I will explain some things in detail concerning their existence, but first there are only a few more things I want to cover in reference to apostleship over the next two chapters.

The Seal, The Signs, & The Mysteries of Apostles

Over the next two chapters, I will be examining additional factors that identify an apostle as an apostle. The difference is that the administrations that we've examined in the previous chapter deal with how the apostolic mantle functions at its core. However, what I will cover over the next two chapters depict the additional works and attributes recognized of the apostle as they are indeed functioning within their administrations.

The Seal

1 Corinthians 9:2
If I be not an apostle unto others, yet doubtless I am to you: for the seal of mine apostleship are ye in the Lord.

In 1 Corinthians 9:2, the word seal literally means authentication, however the root word means to enclose or to fence in.

This means that the authentication of an apostle is what actually provides the protection to the ones who are covered under their apostleship.

With this in mind, we should next understand that the seal of apostleship and the signs of the apostle go hand in hand, but are not necessarily the same.

The signs are the supernatural works that the apostles accomplish and the seal is the results that the particular works have in the lives of the people, or in a particular region, and lastly the covering that comes as a result (See also 2 Corinthians 10:12-18).

The Signs: Marks of an Apostle

2 Corinthians 12:12
Truly the signs of an apostle were wrought among you in all patience, in signs, and wonders, and mighty deeds.

I want to reiterate that the signs of the apostle are not merely signs and wonders, but rather there are many other works to consider as signs of an apostle other than signs and wonders. The scripture is actually saying that all of the works that signify an apostle are wrought and produced in signs and wonders.

In other words, the works of an apostle require the supernatural power of God in demonstration as a testament of the apostolic in action. This is what 2 Corinthians 12:12 is giving us insight into. Therefore, we understand that there are many scriptures that should be considered in identifying the actual works of an apostle.

In fact, the word "sign" in 2 Corinthians 12:12 is actually defined as a "mark". Furthermore, the "marks" of an apostle are things that we can readily notice in order to examine and verify whether an individual is a legitimate apostle or not.

This is key because many self-called apostles assume that their intrusion into the office exempts them of any type of examination. On the contrary, the apostolic is an office that Jesus Himself instructs us to assess in order to validate its authenticity according to Revelations 2:2.

We are not to just accept an individual as an apostle just because they have the title on their websites, flyers, business cards, and social media profiles. In fact, true apostles do not mind the high level of scrutiny that the scriptures reflect being associated to the office. Such does not intimidate them because they understand how their mantles rise to the occasion of such demands to validate its potency.

With that in mind I want to take a moment and list various basic works that identify and marks apostleship. Afterwards, throughout the next chapter, I will deal with three basic attributes of apostleship that rather bring about diversity within the apostolic office, which are as follows: their mystery, their measure, and their maturity.

12 Basic Works of an Apostle

1) Advancing the kingdom within every social & governmental system (Matthew 24:14; Mark 16:15)

2) Laboring & travailing in prayer (Colossians 4:12; Galatians 4:19)

3) Mass Evangelism & Birthing Churches (Matthew 9:37-38; Acts 2:41; Acts 4:4)

4) Establishing/Confirming New Converts in the Faith (Acts 8:14-17; Acts 15:30-35)

5) Opening Economies to Resource the Church (Acts 4:34-35)

6) Imparting Gifts Necessary to the Edifying of the Church (Romans 1:11)

7) Governing Gifts (I Corinthians 14)

8) Bringing Order, Correction, & Discipline within the Church (1 Corinthians 5:1-8; 2 Corinthians 2:1-11)

9) Training the Believer for Ministry (Ephesians 4:11-12)

10) Spiritual Parenting (1 Corinthians 4:15-17; 1 Timothy 1:2)

11) Defending the Faith (Philippians 1:7, 16-17)

12) Mediating & Deliberating with Kings & Royal Delegates Concerning the Advancement of God's Kingdom (Acts 26:2-3; Acts 23:24; Acts 24:24)

Keep in mind that the previous are but a very few examples of an apostle's works. There are multiple other examples that can be found in the New Testament.

However, I want to now begin to deal with three basic attributes of the apostolic mantle that bring about diversity in apostolic expression and authority. What I mean by this is that every apostle is not on the same level.

Some apostles are just awakening while others have already ascended into various spheres of authority. I call recognize these three basics as attributes because they are elements that should verifiable at some level no matter what stage of apostleship they may be in.

I will deal with one now and cover the other two over the next chapter. They are as follows: The Mystery, The Measure, and The Maturity.

The Mystery

Ephesians 3:3-5
How that by revelation he made known unto me the mystery; (as I wrote afore in few words, (4) Whereby, when ye read, ye may understand my knowledge in the mystery of Christ) (5) Which in other ages was not made known unto the sons of men, as it is now revealed unto his holy apostles and prophets by the Spirit;

The mystery of the apostle is pertaining to the specific special message they have been called and chosen to champion. This is where apostolic expression becomes extremely diverse because each apostle's grace is centered on the main message that God anoints them to deliver to the body of Christ and the world at large.

However, we must not get into a spirit of error concerning heaven's mysteries. And what I mean by this is that we are living in a time in which everyone feels as if they have a new revelation. Preachers are literally conjuring up strange revelations in an attempt to appear to others that they are the next best thing that people should give ear to.

On the contrary, every special message of a true apostle will never deviate from the foundational truths and basic doctrines found in Hebrews 6:1-5. And you'd be surprised how many profess to be apostles and do not understand some of the elementary principals of our faith mentioned in Hebrews 6 such as water baptism, repentance, the power of the Holy Ghost, and other foundational truths.

The truth is that every true apostle is well versed in fundamental truths. And it doesn't matter how far away our culture moves away from the scripture, the foundations of God's church will be preserved in the apostolic anointing.

The Power in Simplicity

The thing that keeps apostles acclimated to high levels of revelation is the fact that they are deeply rooted in the practicalities of stewarding great power. They never teach to prove a point or show off their latest biblical studies.

In fact, apostles are just as committed in teaching the basic doctrines as they are in campaigning the church's pivotal and transitional messages. They will never forsake the basics and because of it they are not interested in delegating the responsibility of foundational teaching to the "Sunday School Department".

I believe that one of the safest places for those acclimated to the high-powered revelations of the apostolic is found in simplicity. And trust me, as someone who has written 6 books over the last 2 years, I'm definitely speaking from experience here.

There is a way to be simple without becoming shallow. It's possible to be practical and remain powerful.

One of the most powerful things about the message an apostle carries is in the fact that they are not in a pursuit of "being deep". However, their depth of revelation is often noticed in their ability to take a scripture that is relatively known and widely acknowledged and pull out of it heaven's hidden secrets (Matthew 11:25-27).

This is exactly what Peter did in the upper as he preached on the day of Pentecost. He was able to take an ancient scripture that all were familiar with, use it to explain a modern move of God that all were unfamiliar with, and do so without deviating from the integrity of his chosen text.

In Defense of the Gospel

Another key component to consider concerning an apostle's mystery is its defense. This is significant because if global concerns arise and an individual is not able to give an answer to the concern with biblical clarity then it is proof that they are not apostolic (1 Peter 3:5). If the public misrepresents the church and an individual is not able to biblically defend the faith then they are not apostolic (Philippians 1:7, 16-17).

Philippians 1:7, 16-17

*Even as it is meet for me to think this of you all, because I have you in my heart; inasmuch as both in my bonds, and in the defence and confirmation of the gospel, ye all are partakers of my grace.
(16) The one preach Christ of contention, not sincerely, supposing to add affliction to my bonds:
(17) But the other of love, knowing that I am set for the defence of the gospel.*

I want to take a closer look at Philippians because therein is a powerful truth pertaining to apostleship. It not only confirms the apostle's commitment to their message, but it also reveals how the apostolic mantle acts to guard the message that the apostle is called to carry.

The truth is that if anything arises that tries to skew people's perspective of who Jesus really is, apostles are set as a defense against it. When things are conspired to discredit the church and its leadership, apostles are set as a defense against it.

It's one thing to understand that apostles are messengers, and to embrace that there is no way around it. But another dimension of the apostolic is revealed when we understand not only that apostles are messengers, but also that the apostolic mantle literally acts to break down every contradiction to its message.

It is in fact by way of the apostolic anointing that the world begins to understand that there is no wisdom, understanding, or counsel against the Lord according to Proverbs 21:30. The apostolic mantle literally leaves no room for the theologies and philosophies of other dead religions to coexist with the gospel.

Neither does it allow the attention of individuals towards its message to be derailed by impostors. This is why the angel came to slay the king Herod in Acts 12:19-24.

Herod didn't understand the difference in persecuting Peter and getting away with it, as opposed to the consequences that come when attempting to steal the glory that belongs to God.

And lets not forget about when the sorcerer was blinded by God because he tried to hinder Paul's message (Acts 13:8-12). And when the high priest commanded that Paul be smote in the mouth because of his preaching (Acts 23:2)?

Paul's response was that God would smite the high priest (Acts 23:3). And you know what? I believe God indeed smote that man.

You see, as apostles, we must be harmless as doves and rejoice in persecution, but that does not mean that there are not consequences for trying to stop the message of Kingdom and the works of God (Matthew 5:10-12; Matthew 10:16).

The difference is that an apostle should be willing to suffer persecution for the message that they carry. Individuals will come against them and try to stop them for the message they preach, and true apostles suffer such in humility willing that the individuals ultimately come to repentance.

But when an individual crosses the line and intentionally attempts to stop the work of God, the individual is no longer just in the category of a persecutor, but rather in the category of an enemy who absurdly attempts to fight against God (Acts 5:34-42). And the hard truth is that God will at times move individuals out of the way who are hindering thousands or even potentially millions of others from being rescued out of the grips of hell's fire.

According to Philippians 1:7, 16-17 and Mark 16:20 these things are signs that confirm the message of an apostle. They are just as much as signs as raising the dead and healing the sick.

However, the message of an apostle is not the only thing that we must consider. The next thing that we should in fact evaluate is where their message derives from.

Visions & Revelations

2 Corinthians 12:1

It is not expedient for me doubtless to glory. I will come to visions and revelations of The Lord.

Apostles have a high capacity for revelation because of the fact that all of their messages derive from the world that they are ambassadors of, which is heaven. For this reason, it is not abnormal for them to be given a direct message from Jesus Himself or one if His assigned angelic delegates.

I strongly recommend that you read my book *Jesus in HD* because in it I deal with multiple levels of revelation that apostles, and not only apostles, but everybody can access in the realms of the Spirit. However, in this book I will briefly cover two things as it pertains to revelation.

1) The Revelation of Jesus Christ

Galatians 1:11-12
But I certify you, brethren, that the gospel which was preached of me is not after man. For I neither received it of man, neither was I taught it, but by the revelation of Jesus Christ.

1 Corinthians 9:1
Am I not an apostle? Am I not free? Have I not seen Jesus Christ our Lord? are not ye my work in the Lord?

The revelation of Jesus is when an apostle encounters the Lord face to face and is sent with a specific message directly from Jesus. I reiterate that apostles are those who are sent from the face of Jesus. This means that an apostle's mandate and assignment usually comes from an encounter that they have had with Jesus.

You can read more about visitations from the Lord in my book *Jesus in HD (High Demand)* and also my book *Experiencing God in the Supernatural Newly Revised*. In this book I want to more so focus on the revelation of God's counsel.

2) The Counsel/Council of God

Acts 2:23
Him, being delivered by the determinate counsel and foreknowledge of God, ye have taken, and by wicked hands have crucified and slain:

First, let me explain that the council of God is in reference to a company of governing and judicial elders in the heavens. However, the counsel of God is rather the wisdom that comes forth from within this company.

Acts 2:23 is proof that apostles have access into God's counsel by way of His council. Just as the prophets of old, apostles are invited in on heaven's board meetings in which they may interact with several different delegates of God's council staff.

How else would Peter have had insight into such facts surrounding the death and resurrection of Jesus that scriptures prior never mentions Jesus disclosing to His apostles? Could this be info that was relayed in the board meeting that took place on the mount of transfiguration between Jesus, Elijah, and Moses (Luke 9:28-35)?

There are obviously decisions that are not made in heaven apart from the input of God's council. It's not that God actually needs counsel, but rather He demonstrates His commitment to His own wisdom in merely the existence of the 24 elders that surround His throne (Revelations 4:4).

We may not have complete insight into this phenomenon, but we do have scriptural proof of its existence. Furthermore, by way of revelatory experience and various tracked evidence and examples from God's word this mystery begins to unfold to us the more.

The truth is that as we ascend the ranks of heaven, there are various dignitaries of the Kingdom that they we become acquainted with. Evidence of this is seen as Ezekiel experiences various angelic escorts that begin to grant him entrance and transport throughout various realms of the Spirit (Ezekiel 3, 8, 11, 37, 40, 41, & 44).

This was also evident in the life of Daniel in how he had begun to interact with the watchers of heaven who make decrees that enforce heaven's rule within the kingdoms of men in the earth (Daniel 4:13-17). By the way, don't forget about Daniel's collaborate with Michael the archangel in the overthrowing of the demonic prince of Persia, and these are just a few (Daniel 10:10-14).

I know that this is a deep teaching and frankly there is no way around it, and no way to water it down. After all, this is a book on the apostolic. However, I would admonish you to do more study on the throne room of God and His governing council before ever and I mean ever trying to relay such a truth to others in greater detail.

When it's all said and done, the message that I'm trying to convey is that apostles are very acclimated to heaven and accustomed to interacting with heaven's highest delegates and officials. This is significant because there are certain prophetic revelations that do not come forth apart from God's council.

The prophets of old are a testament of this reality. In fact, Jeremiah 23:21-23 consists of a rebuke to the prophets who attempt to prophesy having never stood among God's council. Lets take a look at this and briefly dissect in as we conclude our journey into understanding this truth.

Jeremiah 23:21-23
I have not sent these prophets, yet they ran: I have not spoken to them, yet they prophesied. But if they had stood in my counsel, and had caused my people

to hear my words, then they should have turned them from their evil way, and from the evil of their doings. Am I a God at hand, saith the Lord, and not a God afar off?

The word counsel in the text literally means a session with a company of persons. And according to the book of Hebrews this company could consist of the Lord Jesus, His angels, the elders, or even the spirits of just men made perfect (Hebrews 12:22-29).

In the counsel of the Lord there are a series of divine encounters that often include angelic messages, angelic escorts, angelic assistance, and angelic reinforcement. I want to reiterate that this takes place as we are introduced to multiple dignitaries and representatives of God's Kingdom to the extent that they may readily assist us in either fully comprehending or executing the revelation granted to us.

In fact, this is exactly what happened to John in the book of Revelations. At one minute he is at the throne of God and the next he is talking with one the 24 elders.

One minute, there is one of the living creatures engaging him, and in the next, angels. He's hearing voices, seeing visions, and the list goes on and on.

I wanted to emphasize the counsel of the Lord because standing in His counsel is different from having an encounter with Jesus. It is coming to heaven's round table and being granted a judicial position among heaven's courts.

This is in fact the level of revelation and authority that Peter preached with on the day of Pentecost according to Acts 2:23. We should never reduce this type of preaching to merely being the effective delivery of a sermon.

No seminary or bible college can cause this grace to sit on an individual's message. The practicing of "preaching skills" definitely will not make it happen.

We sadly live in a generation of individuals who put great effort into making their voices sound more powerful than their message truly is. But when it's all said and done this type of apostolic preaching power can only be given from heaven.

When apostles open up the mysteries of the Spirit in their preaching, we should be aware that the heavens are leaning in, the angels are assessing, and life-altering decisions are being made. This is but a small glimpse into the power of an apostolic message.

However, based on what we have learned so far, when an individual professes to be an apostle we could then ask the following questions: What is their message, and whom did they get the message from? Are they solid in foundational truths, and does their message prove to be pivotal for the church?

What revelatory clarity does their message bring, and how does it help its listeners guard against the erred teachings of heretics? And finally, if they pass the litmus test concerning apostolic mysteries, the next thing we should examine is their apostolic measure.

Apostolic Measures & Maturity

The Measure

2 Corinthians 10:12-18
For we dare not make ourselves of the number, or compare ourselves with some that commend themselves: but they measuring themselves by themselves, and comparing themselves among themselves, are not wise. (13) But we will not boast of things without our measure, but according to the <u>measure of the rule</u>, which God hath distributed to us, <u>a measure to reach even unto you</u>. (14) For we stretch not ourselves beyond our measure, as though we reached not unto you: for we are come as far as to you also in preaching the gospel of Christ: (15) Not boasting of things without our measure, that is, of other men's labours; but having hope, when your faith is increased, that we shall be enlarged by you according to our rule abundantly, (16) To preach the gospel in the regions beyond you, and not to boast in another man's line of things made ready to our hand. (17) But he that glorieth, let him glory in the Lord. (18) For not he that commendeth himself is approved, but whom the Lord commendeth.

The measure of rule in the scripture speaks to the reach of an apostle's mantle. Does it extend over small groups, or does it extend over regions, or even nations? This is key because the weight of an apostle's message will often depend on the extent of their measure.

If an apostle has not been expanded to a place of where their measure of rule is extending over nations their message will in turn most likely not address global concerns. However, this does not diminish the authority that they have in their particular sphere, whether it be small or large.

Another key concerning an apostle's measure of rule is that it does not deal with merely any type of reach, but rather a spiritual reach. This means that an individual can be on every Christian television station there is and still have no valid measure of rule.

The measure of rule more specifically deals with the number of individuals whom the apostle's ministry actually brings and sustains transformation in their lives. It is extremely powerful, because an apostle's measure of rule can extend over thousands upon thousands of individuals. However, we must not mistake earthly success with kingdom success as it pertains to reaching the great multitudes of people.

An individual can be reaching hundreds of thousands of people. Maybe they have a church of 5,000, but the only problem is that 4,999 of them are devils. Or maybe they have 13,000 on the role, but only 1,300 show on Sunday, and that's only if you count all three services.

That's clearly not apostolic. However, a true apostle's measure of rule is very serious business and they are very well apt to identify such. Paul demonstrates this truth very well in his writings to the Corinthians.

1 Corinthians 9:2
If I be not an apostle unto others, yet doubtless I am to you: for the seal of mine apostleship are ye in the Lord.

I think it is also important to clarify that an apostle's reach is not based on how many people merely repeat the sinner's prayer, but rather how many are actually being cultivated and matured under their apostleship. In the end, apostles don't attempt to make their ministries seem more impactful than they really are.

Apostles are delivered from what I call the "evangelistic exaggeration disease". It's a disease that causes ministers to project their ministries as accomplishing more than it truly is. When you are delivered from this severe illness you are content with the reach of your ministry whether it be to 5 or 5,000.

However, on the contrary, apostles do they make excuses for their ministries either remaining small or lacking progress. A true apostle embraces the fact that it is built into the very nature of their mantles for their reach to be ever expanding.

Apostles have an attractional force in their mantles that draws individuals by the multitudes into the Kingdom of God. This is why when Peter preached in the upper room, an immediate 3,000 were added to the church.

In fact, following the 3,000 that were added to the church in Acts 2:41, there were another 5,000 added in Acts 4:4. And by the time the scripture reaches Acts 6:7, the church was growing so much that they just stopped counting. Scripture only records that their numbers multiplied GREATLY.

Acts 6: 7
And the word of God increased; and the number of the disciples multiplied in Jerusalem greatly; and a great company of the priests were obedient to the faith.

This is significant to me for two reasons. One is that whenever the scriptures numbered the multitude it was not counting the women and children.

This is significant because there has always been a greater ratio of women to men. This means that if there were 5,000 men present there had to be anywhere from 10,000-15,000 individuals present in all at minimal.

The second reason that Acts 6:7 is significant to me is that it was the closest that the book of Acts show the apostles reaching multitudes in the same manner that Jesus was in Luke 12:1. Let's take a look.

Luke 12:1
In the mean time, when there were gathered together an innumerable multitude of people, insomuch that they trode one upon another, he began to say unto his disciples first of all, Beware ye of the leaven of the Pharisees, which is hypocrisy.

The revelation is in the word innumerable. The word literally means that there were too many people to count.

This means that in Acts 6:7, if the number of men had multiplied to the extent to where they just stopped counting, how many more women and children do you think were present? You do the math and you will understand that the possibilities of whole nations being converted are not so far stretched after all.

Apostles understand what Jesus meant when He taught them that the harvest was plentiful and that they should press into that reality, not just to build a mega church, but until they see whole cities and even whole nations changed (Matthew 9:37; Acts 8:5-17; Acts 19:10). I know that this is not the only thing that an apostle's measure represents; it's just the portion that I've been led of God to pen so far.

However, the diversity that comes in an apostle's measure is in the truth that every apostle is not called to the same sphere. Neither does every apostle carry the same weight in the Spirit. In fact, there are some teachers that may carry more weight than some apostles depending on their measure.

Some apostles are missionaries while others are stationary. Some are the senior leaders of local congregations while others rather oversee multiple congregations within their jurisdiction. Therefore, if an individual is being recognized as an apostle the next questions we would need to ask is what are they an apostle over and who are they an apostle to?

What spheres are they assigned to and what have they established in that sphere? Who does their mantle attract; new converts or the typical "church groupie"? What have they planted and caused to flourish from its ground roots, and in what spheres do they exercise governing and legislative authority?

The Maturity

Maturity is key because our character must correspond with the mighty works of God through us in ways that are complimentary as opposed to distasteful. What I mean by this is that it does not matter if we can prophesy accurately if we are rude, and it does not matter if we can raise the dead if we've lost our integrity.

The church will understand this more as we get to the place where we are just as impressed with the fruit of the Spirit, as we are the gifts of the Spirit. We must remember that one of the first things that Jesus taught the apostles were the beatitudes (Matthew 5).

He was teaching them the lifestyle of the kingdom because only it can bear up under the true power and weight of the Kingdom. The power of God can be rather detrimental in the lives of those who are not processed in integrity. This is why the beginning lessons and foundational teaching of Jesus to the original 12 apostles were in subjects of meekness, hunger after righteousness, joy in persecution, and the like.

If there was anything that I could leave in a nutshell concerning these matters it would be that the essentials of kingdom character are forged in humility, servant hood, and overcoming trials. A person who claims to be an apostle without these three very evident in their lives, they are nothing less than tyrants and egotistic maniacs in the making. The only safeguard is that we, as an apostolic community, must become as well versed in the scriptures pertaining to purity and practicality in our lifestyles to the same extent that we are versed in scriptures pertaining to faith, power, glory, authority, the supernatural and the likes.

The diversity in this is in the sobering reality that yes, there are some crazy "apostles gone wild" out there. Yes, I said it, and might I add that there are some false ones as well. And frankly they often make us all look bad due to their immaturity.

However, you cannot throw the baby out with the bathwater, neither should we associate the real with the fake. Just know that it is a definite red flag whenever an individual's claims of power, and almost "hustle-like grind" in ministry is more evident than their character and integrity. Jesus said that you would know them by their fruit.

Therefore, when an individual professes to be an apostle we should then ask the question, what is their fruit? Are they mean, snappy, or arrogant? If they're married, how do they treat their spouse?

Do they pay their bills on time? Do they have a work ethic? Are they accountable to anyone, and can anyone unapologetically correct them? The list goes on and on...

Why Maturity?

Great suffering is a prerequisite of great glory according to Romans 8:18, which is one of the reasons that the maturity of an apostle is paramount. The character of an apostle has to be unquestionable because of the trials its mantle attracts.

If an individual's integrity level is not intact within an office as such, they will literally break under the pressure that the weight of the apostolic anointing applies. Ascending into apostleship is like the enlisting into the marine corps of the United States military branches. Its initiation process will consist of the hardest and the toughest boot camp due to the threats that it will inevitably face afterwards...

According to 1 Corinthians 4:9, even the angels that are assigned to the mantle are rigorous towards the individuals who are being inducted into its services. It is definitely not for the weak.

Therefore, before concluding this chapter, I want to take a moment to list only a very few among many scriptures that depict the sufferings of an apostle. Prayerfully, not only will we gain a greater respect for those who are called to the apostolic, considering what they must endure, but also those who are so eager to join the ranks of an apostle will think twice about assuming an office that they have not be called and graced to stand in.

1 Corinthians 4:9-14
For I think that God hath set forth us the apostles last, as it were appointed to death: for we are made a spectacle unto the world, and to angels, and to men. (10) We are fools for Christ's sake, but ye are wise in Christ; we are weak, but ye are strong; ye are honourable, but we are despised. (11) Even unto this present hour we both hunger, and thirst, and are naked, and are buffeted, and have no

certain dwellingplace; (12) And labour, working with our own hands: being reviled, we bless; being persecuted, we suffer it: (13) Being defamed, we intreat: we are made as the filth of the world, and are the offscouring of all things unto this day. (14) I write not these things to shame you, but as my beloved sons I warn you.

2 Corinthians 6:3-10
Giving no offence in any thing, that the ministry be not blamed: (4) But in all things approving ourselves as the ministers of God, in much patience, in afflictions, in necessities, in distresses, (5) In stripes, in imprisonments, in tumults, in labours, in watchings, in fastings; (6) By pureness, by knowledge, by longsuffering, by kindness, by the Holy Ghost, by love unfeigned, (7) By the word of truth, by the power of God, by the armour of righteousness on the right hand and on the left, (8) By honour and dishonour, by evil report and good report: as deceivers, and yet true; (9) As unknown, and yet well known; as dying, and, behold, we live; as chastened, and not killed; (10) As sorrowful, yet alway rejoicing; as poor, yet making many rich; as having nothing, and yet possessing all things.

2 Corinthians 11:23-31
Are they ministers of Christ? (I speak as a fool) I am more; in labours more abundant, in stripes above measure, in prisons more frequent, in deaths oft. (24) Of the Jews five times received I forty stripes save one. (25) Thrice was I beaten with rods, once was I stoned, thrice I suffered shipwreck, a

night and a day I have been in the deep; (26) In journeyings often, in perils of waters, in perils of robbers, in perils by mine own countrymen, in perils by the heathen, in perils in the city, in perils in the wilderness, in perils in the sea, in perils among false brethren; (27) In weariness and painfulness, in watchings often, in hunger and thirst, in fastings often, in cold and nakedness. (28) Beside those things that are without, that which cometh upon me daily, the care of all the churches. (29) Who is weak, and I am not weak? who is offended, and I burn not? (30) If I must needs glory, I will glory of the things which concern mine infirmities. (31) The God and Father of our Lord Jesus Christ, which is blessed for evermore, knoweth that I lie not.

Conclusion

Please keep in mind that the previous are only a very basic list of things that mark apostleship. There are many things that could be learned concerning apostles, but my assignment in this book is only to lay the foundation necessary for expounding upon the apostolic centers that will emerge in this next season. I believe at this point we are ready to move forward.

The Antioch Pattern for Apostolic Centers

There are many movements on the forefront of what the church knows today as revival. You have the prayer/worship movement, the healing movement, and movements of evangelism/ harvesting. There is also a surge of marketplace ministry, the word of faith's prosperity movement, as well as a movement of insight into just practical everyday living.

However, in this next movement in which apostolic centers will emerge, all of these movements, along with other added graces, will converge together constituting one global move. Therefore, apostolic centers will not only have emphasis on the apostolic and prophetic, but also have a high emphasis on healing, prayer, evangelism, market place ministry, prosperity, and last but not least, everyday practicality.

Sad to say, the apostles of our time have been so focused on revelations of what they believe the apostolic is that they have forgotten that the apostles of old were on the forefront of the previously mentioned efforts.

They were on the front lines of prayer, and they were the first to be found passionately pursuing the presence of the Lord. They didn't delegate the burdens of intercession to the so-called "prayer warriors" of the church. They always demonstrated the power of God and when they evangelized souls were saved in mass numbers.

Furthermore, the bulk of their evangelism took place in the leading markets of their day as opposed to merely within the confines of "Sunday morning church". They had an ability to open up economies and lastly, because of their ability to practically articulate the depths of God without compromising truth, their ministry was just as effective in dealing with unbelievers as it was in dealing with the church.

Although apostolic centers will constitute more than the previous they will not be any less efficient than the leading ministries of our day who pioneer in the charismatic and Pentecostal movements of worship, prayer, evangelism, power healing & deliverance, prosperity, market place ministry, discipleship, and practical everyday living.

Laying the Foundation

With the previous in mind lets begin our journey in understanding what an apostolic center consists of by taking a look into various key scriptures predominately within Acts 15. The leadership structure of the church within this whole chapter is important to consider because of how the church had begun to expand from Judea at that point towards Antioch...

You would have to refer to Acts 1:8 again in reference to the church's expansion in order for this to make sense.

Acts 1:8
But ye shall receive power, after that the Holy Ghost is come upon you: and ye shall be witnesses unto me both in Jerusalem, and in all Judaea, and in Samaria, and unto the uttermost part of the earth.

I want to reiterate that in Acts 1:8, Jesus does not only promise power, but He also gives the church a preview of how it would progress to advance God's Kingdom in the earth beginning at Jerusalem and then spreading throughout the entire world.

By the time the book of Acts lands in chapter 15 and the expansion promised in Acts 1:8 had already been in effect for some time, we also notice that the church's leadership structure had begun to adjust in order accommodate its progress. In fact, there were three major leadership shifts in the book of Acts by the time we reach Acts 15.

This is where the church is once again prophetically. Furthermore, we can take a look at Acts 6:1 in order to notice what takes place when the church advances but the administration remains the same. There are consequences for not shifting with the current moves of God.

Acts 6:1
And in those days, when the number of the disciples was multiplied, there arose a murmuring of the Grecians against the Hebrews, because their widows were neglected in the daily ministration.

We see clearly that as the church began to grow there was a need for a different "(ad)ministration" to be set in place. And remember, the apostolic mantle is conditioned to provide solutions for such.

However, the scripture shows clearly that when the administration of the church does not progress along with the church's forward movement, it can cause the people to be left in a place of unrest. Many are frustrated in the body of Christ even now because they know that there is more but they don't quite know how to access it.

This is one of the reasons why God is raising up apostolic centers today. There is a fresh move of God in the earth today that is requiring systems and models to be put in place in order to steward its progression. Our times are calling for a specific type of apostolic administration and I believe the Antioch church of Acts 15 gives great insight into that administration.

I also believe that there are some basics concerning the nature of apostolic centers that can be discovered not only in the study in Acts 15, but also in the history of how the church of Antioch came into existence. Let's take a moment and examine some historical facts concerning the church at Antioch.

Basic Historical Facts of Antioch

Antioch is 1st mentioned in Acts 6:5 & Acts 11:19 prior to Acts 13 and Acts 15. Therefore, there are two historical facts I would like to pull from Acts 6 and Acts 11 that will give us clarity into how the leadership construct of Acts 13 and Acts 15 came into play.

1) The church was birthed not only in great growth, but also in great persecution (Acts 6:5, 7)

It was after the church had multiplied greatly that persecution hit causing some to spread as far as Antioch.

I believe this fact is prophetically significant because it meant that the Antioch church was conditioned to be the apostolic headquarters they were as they embraced both the upside and the downside of ministry.

This is key because the ones who are attracted to the ministry only for the "lights, cameras, and action" will not make this next shift. Those who want to use the pulpit in order to become popular and make a name for themselves will be excluded as well. Yes, there will be those that come into great influence and reputation. However, it will only be those whose character and motive has been properly prepared to bear the weight of responsibility that comes along with that.

One thing for sure, apostolic centers are born in the midst of adversity, and unrest, and turmoil. In fact, certain apostolic administrations only emerge in times of great controversy. Sometimes the right friction has to be applied in order to aggravate the apostolic mantle into action.

2) An Apostolic Center is a Place of Convergence and Alliance (Acts 11:22, 25-27)

Acts 11:22, 25-27
Then tidings of these things came unto the ears of the church which was in Jerusalem: and they sent forth Barnabas, that he should go as far as Antioch. (25) Then departed Barnabas to Tarsus, for to seek Saul: (26) And when he had found him, he brought him unto Antioch. And it came to pass, that a whole year they assembled themselves with the church, and taught much people. And the disciples were called Christians first in Antioch. (27) And in these days came prophets from Jerusalem unto Antioch.

According to vs. 25-26 of the text, I believe that Antioch represents the place where alliances are formed. It's also the place where apostolic ministry evolves and the next leaders who are called to be on the front lines are cultivated and launched. And according to vs. 27, it's the place where the old and new converge as well as the pace where the apostolic and prophetic converge.

However, more specifically, the connection of Saul and Barnabas is a great example of the alliance needed in order for an apostolic center to emerge. It is very significant because Barnabas had a place among the apostolic council at Jerusalem, which consisted of the church's founding apostles. Saul, however, did not have the seat of authority that Barnabas did although he was yet carrying the baton for the next move of God.

The prophetic significance of such is that there are literally modern ministries that have been strong and established for years that are seemingly struggling. Why? The answer is that God is requiring that the hearts of fathers and sons be turned towards each other (Malachi 4:6). We will need both the wisdom of the old order and the strength of the new order to converge in order to successfully progress. And I do not mention this in reference to age but rather in reference to the Lord's timing in raising an individual up upon a major platform.

Jonathan Ferguson

The Antioch Pattern

I couldn't reiterate enough how important the Antioch pattern is. It is the very first time in scripture that we see a council of apostles and other fivefold leaders actually governing the forward progression of the church after Pentecost.

You see, it's one thing to try to partner with other ministries and unify the body of Christ, but it's another thing to actually understand the logistics included in effectively fostering the emergence of such a church.

I reiterate that the things that took place leading to the church at Antioch coming into existence brought about major leadership shifts. The shifts were so drastic in that the church leadership was first noticed voting for their next leaders in Acts 1:24-26. But by the time we reach Acts 13:1 the leaders are not voting, they are praying and fasting together.

Notice that the leaders present in Acts 13:1 did not initially convene to debate doctrines, neither are they jockeying positions. They were humbling themselves in prayer and not interested in the attempt of hustling their way to the top of the "ministry food chain". Antioch was not a pastor's retreat where they gleaned great ideas on how to write better sermons or patronize each other for more preaching engagements.

Something powerful is taking place at Antioch. The leadership of the church is actually lying down on their faces together before the Lord. They didn't have "head intercessors" that they were willing to email their prayer concerns to rather than pray themselves.

Antioch was a place where the Holy Ghost brought about the unity necessary for next level leadership because He found a nucleus of individuals that would lie down on their faces until He called the shots. And when the Holy Ghost spoke they didn't all have their own personal interpretations and opinions of what was spoken. They all heard the same word at the same time so that there was no question concerning what God was truly saying.

The church was growing too rapidly for the leadership to become the cause of souls, newly saved, to be led astray. And there was so much persecution and trial that the leadership couldn't afford to make the wrong moves due to lack of relying on the Lord's direction or maybe an overconfidence in their own wisdom.

The Antioch leadership had an ability to submit themselves to The Lord in seeking His will. And they didn't mind being accountable to each other in the process of doing so.

The results of such were that a powerful church began to emerge, and its no coincidence that believers were first called Christians at

Antioch. However, I don't want to imply that apostolic centers are going to become the new way of doing church. It is a leadership model.

Not every local church will be required to model everything that the Antioch church represents, however I believe that regional gatherings will be hosted by leaders who have formed an alliance in order to adopt the Antioch pattern of ministry in ways that could provide services to the local congregations of a particular region. With that in mind lets now dissect from Acts 15 what the Antioch model of apostolic leadership exists to accomplish in the church and in doing so we will understand what an apostolic centers is.

Emerging Apostolic Centers

One of the most significant things concerning the Antioch church is that it was modeled after the tabernacle of David according to Acts 15:16. Therefore, there is a lot we can learn of an apostolic center from what its construction represented.

Acts 15:16-17
After this I will return, and will build again the tabernacle of David, which is fallen down; and I will build again the ruins thereof, and I will set it up: That the residue of men might seek after the Lord, and all the Gentiles, upon whom my name is called, saith the Lord, who doeth all these things.

In short, David's tabernacle was a place where prophetic revelation was given as the people were in a place of worship. It was the place of the manifest presence of the Lord. I expound a lot more on the David's Tabernacle concept in my book *Jesus in HD (High Demand)*.

There are also countless other articles, books, and teaching about the Tabernacle of David that would probably be very beneficial to study out. However, the simple truth that I want to convey from the model of David's Tabernacle is how apostolic centers are presence driven instead of personality driven.

This is why and how the construct of David's Tabernacle allows for the leadership administration alliance necessary to push the church. The leaders are less likely to deal with ego issues and selfish ministry ambitions because they are not in it to attract a following to themselves.

Their hearts are to pursue the Lord and to propel His church and not merely their individual ministries. These qualities are very imperative when building a team council leadership structure.

The leadership's main objective is to lead the people into the presence of the Lord and receive His strategy to advance God's Kingdom. As a result, there is great harvesting, and many souls are saved as the church implements heaven's current strategy of advancing the Kingdom of God in the earth.

Sometimes we get so apostolic that we forget that the main objective is that people truly encounter Jesus and that souls are saved. However, apostolic centers are nothing less than revival centers, they are power centers, and they exist as regional kingdom headquarters. In fact, whatever you choose to call the gathering is fine as long as they are operating in ways that advance the Kingdom of God.

And please do not feel compelled to "tag" apostolic center onto your church's name. If your church's name is Abundant Life, it does NOT have to become Abundant Life Apostolic Center.

And I reiterate that every church does not have to become one, neither did every local assembly represent such throughout the New Testament scriptures. However, believers everywhere will be affected by their emergence.

How an Apostolic Center's Leadership is Structured

Acts 15:22
Then pleased it the apostles and elders, with the whole church, to send chosen men of their own company to Antioch with Paul and Barnabas; namely, Judas surnamed Barsabas, and Silas, chief men among the brethren:

I believe, in addition to souls being saved, one of the most impactful things about an apostolic center is how various leaders from their various spheres converge together in one place in order to advance the Kingdom in a specific region. Acts 15:35 verifies that this team ministry is indeed modeled before the people.

This may seem very minute, but in actuality, there are systems that are required to be in place in order to accomplish a specific set of objectives required for this to take place. Therefore, I want to progress by quickly highlighting some of the main features of an apostolic center's leadership and governance, and also what exists to campaign as demonstrated by the Antioch church throughout Acts chapters 11-15.

According to Acts 15:22 the leadership structure of an apostolic center is pretty much set up as follows from least authority to the top:

1) Delegate of governing elders
2) Council of 5-fold leaders
3) Chief men among the council (preferably 3)

Now the following are efforts that this apostolic governance exists to accomplish...

10 Foundational Campaigned Emphasis of Apostolic Centers:

1) Strong culture of prayer & worship: The manifest presence and Glory of God

2) The preaching of the kingdom & the supernatural demonstrated in signs, wonders, and miracles

3) Mass evangelism

4) Sound doctrine & the preservation of foundational teaching

5) Team ministry, apostolic council, prophetic round table, & leadership accountability

6) Regional gatherings

7) The clear articulation of universal & absolute standards of the Christian lifestyle

8) Basic focuses of the 5-fold ministry according to Ephesians 4 as follows:
The believer's Identity in Christ
Preparation for ministry
The believer's maturity
The unity of faith
The knowledge of Jesus Christ

9) Proper preparation, endorsement, and a legitimate release of public ministry

10) The establishing of government and helps for the advancement of the kingdom and the growth of the church

NOTE: The final foundational emphasis previously listed requires a discerning of the times along with a constant awareness, understanding, an ability to communicate the current operations and movements of the Spirit, and lastly, multiple periods of performance evaluations and assessments.

Apostolic Center Cliffs Notes

Each of the previous campaigned emphasis of apostolic centers represents a whole world of significance in and of themselves. My suggestion is that you review them again often and as you progress also begin attempting to locate the various qualities throughout the Book of Acts and other New Testament scriptures.

In fact, I'm going to give you access to my cliffs notes as a great example of how you do this. Therefore, at this point I want to focus on Acts 15 and leave you with some things that immediately stand out to me.

However, I will only briefly disclose a few things that the Spirit of God highlighted to me. I want to do so because I believe it can give you an example of how the scriptures should come alive to you in your personal studies of Acts chapters 11-15.

I want to reiterate that the following is in more of a cliff notes style, but I believe you can greatly benefit from me allowing you into my personal notes. I will simply reference the scripture and afterward you should read the scripture while comparing it with my notes.

This is the part where you will need to open your bible. I will not list the scripture as I have done previously.

You will need a King James Bible specifically by the way. I felt led of God to do things this way so that is exactly what I'm going to do.

Here We Go:
Read Acts 15:6

The council at the apostolic center think tanks, hosts prophetic round tables, and from there navigate the issues concerning the church.

They inspect the doctrines & practices of the believers of that region...
They work to set the universal moral code and spiritual standard for the believers to live by (see also Acts 15:5-29)

Read Acts 15:12-13

There is a head for this council...

There are also chief members of the council...

Each chief member of the council has a unique strength.

NOTE: Peter, James, John are great examples...they are historically known as chief among the apostles at Jerusalem. Peter was the voice, John was the most revelatory of the three, but James was head of the council.

This threefold cord was a safety to each of them. Although Peter was the priority spokesman there were decisions that only James was authorized to make within the church. Likewise, I would assume that there was insight into certain decisions to be made that only John had revelation into.

The council was designed to provide an avenue where gifts could converge for greater impact although their individual strengths could stand-alone. In fact, according to Acts 15:12, the fruit of leaders within their individual are often referenced in order to validate their assignment on the council. Furthermore, it would be the fruit of leaders within their own spheres that validates not only their qualification to serve on the council, but as chief among the council.

However, the head of an apostolic council governs to be sure that the influence, the great reputation of an individual, or the mighty works done by those apart of the council does not usurp the authority of the council...

Furthermore, the head of the council is usually not very vocal in the public. Their work is more behind the scenes causing the alliance of the council to not be compromised.

If you think about it, Peter was often in the forefront of the public. Therefore, James heading the council, in the sense of having the right to make final decision in the case of disagreement, provides a safety that doesn't allow Peter to use his public influence to sway the church. Likewise, James not having much of a public voice provides a safety to ensure that internal decisions of the council were not merely to forward advance his individual work.

In other words, although the chief men of the council were most likely second to none in their strengths and were very influential in their various spheres, they did not step outside the confines of their authority among the council. They knew their lanes and stayed within their reach all the while working together for greater kingdom impact and expansion.

Acts 15:40 also gives great insight into how the governing apostolic council of a particular regional apostolic center should be individuals who are endorsed with high recommendation of other influential leaders within the body of Christ.

THE RISK:
What Leaders Fear Most of Team Councils

Read Acts 15:39-40

The contention among leadership, the going of separate ways is the risk of the establishment of apostolic centers that have team councils, BUT VERY MUCH WORTH THE RISK...

However, the good news is that we never have to shy away from this type of leadership structure in fear that someone would capitalize off of our individual graces to their own selfish gain....

If such is attempted we are assured, in Acts 15:39-40, that they will not have the endorsement of respectable leaders in the church, neither will they have the grace on what God has not commissioned them to do...

Many times we are afraid that people will steal our ministry ideas or succeed beyond the place of our own personal success all the while utilizing the very ideas that God has given us to share with them...

The truth is that when there is a mandate that is truly from God, only the person that has been given the mandate has the finisher's grace to actually birth it...a legitimate grace can only be imparted after that point...

This benefits a ministry leader for two reasons: A great idea stolen with the lack of impartation is like a trail that God allows to be traced ultimately exposing the identity theft of impostors...2nd once a legitimate impartation is actually made allowing others to run with the baton you began with, it is not a bad thing...it only frees you up to carry something fresh and something more than you originally carried...

The Verdict: Do what God has given you to do without a fear of sharing with others...you need the strength of others in order to accomplish what God has given you to accomplish in the region you are called to...

Resist the fear and worry that your ministry's uniqueness will be lost in the teamwork and realize that the grace on your life would only be enhanced and sharpened.

Read Acts 15:23-32

Apostolic centers have leaders that establish kingdom headquarters and strongholds in various regions in order to create a network among other leaders and churches.

There is an intertwining of anointing across various states and regions...

Their headquarters become regional churches, and they guard the spiritual gates of the regions that they are established in.

Highlighted Verses:

Vs. 25
When the believers of these regions gather, the eldership of that particular headquarters acts to equip individuals in order to send them back out into the market and into the culture with power and

in purpose...they aim to not only exhort or encourage but to confirm (also see vs.32)

Vs. 30
The leaders gather the multitude...they merge their resources and influence together for the benefit of one joint assignment...

Winding Things Up

Acts 15:40-41
And Paul chose Silas, and departed, being recommended by the brethren unto the grace of God. And he went through Syria and Cilicia, confirming the churches.

Apostolic centers exist as a headquarters capable of sending out apostolic teams to confirm other local assemblies. This is key because the word "confirm" literally means to further support and reestablish.

The apostolic leadership among the council houses a grace to assess local assemblies in order to restructure and reestablish them according to progressive leadership models that are conducive for God's current moves and mandates in their cities and regions.

Conclusion

Advance

This very last truth that I've chosen to pen concerning apostolic centers brings me to one of the main objectives I had in writing this book. I felt an urgency to write this book due to things the Lord has been showing me that He wants to fortify the present day church in so that we not only survive the days to come but thrive in them.

Similar to what took place in the book of Acts, things are changing in our world; the Kingdom of God is advancing, and such will require our leadership models to evolve. And what I mean by evolve is not an attempt at something innovative that we believe to be attractive to public.

I rather mean that we must become more progressive in our understanding of how God is moving and adequately construct avenues through which His movement can be properly expressed. There is an apostolic grace that gets this done.

I know that there are pastors reading this book and I am officially extending my services to you. Even if that only means you only take an initial assessment in order to gather the info required to adequately advise how your ministry could advance from this point.

I'm in alliance with many respectable leaders throughout the body of Christ. We could, at the very least, recommend material that you could outsource. Our resources could prove effective in assisting your church in restructuring.

So if you are a senior leader and anything written in this book tugged on your spirit or awakened in you a desire and hunger for more, please do not hesitate to contact our ministry at www.fergusonsglobal.com. We also have ministry training available for those in preparation to eventually become senior leaders.

God literally dropped this book in my spirit and graced me to complete it in just three weeks and two days, and I know that the Lord had you in mind. Although, our journey in this book ends here, I look forward to hearing from you soon.

In the meantime don't forget to read my book *Jesus in HD (High Demand)*. In it, you will be able to read more testimonies of the fruit that I have seen produced throughout various other ministries and the awakening that I believe the Lord is bringing to your life, your family, your city, your church and your ministry in Jesus name. Amen.

Printed in Great Britain
by Amazon.co.uk, Ltd.,
Marston Gate.